Sea Snails

Science Under The Sea

Lynn M. Stone

Rourke
Publishing LLC
Vero Beach, Florida 32964

PHOTO CREDITS: Cover, p. 7 © Marty Snyderman; title page, p. 10, 20 © James
H. Carmichael; p. 8, 12, 13, 15, 16 © Lynn M. Stone; p. 4, 19 © Brandon Cole.

Cover Photo: *A flamingo tongue snail*

EDITOR: Frank Sloan

COVER DESIGN: Nicola Stratford

Library of Congress Cataloging-in-Publication Data

Stone, Lynn M.
  Sea snails / Lynn M. Stone.
    p. cm. — (Science under the sea)
Summary: Describes the physical characteristics, behavior, and habitat
of these single-shelled sea invertebrates.
Includes bibliographical references (p.   ).
  ISBN 1-58952-320-2 (hardcover)
  1. Snails—Juvenile literature. 2. Marine invertebrates—Juvenile
literature. [1. Snails. 2. Marine invertebrates.] I. Title.
  QL430.4 .S846 2002
  594'.34—dc21
                                                2002005130

Printed in the USA

CG/CG

Table of Contents

Sea Snails

Snails are small, soft, boneless animals with hard shells. Sea snails are the snails that live in the oceans.

Snails belong to the group of animals that scientists call **molluscs**. Most kinds of molluscs have hard shells. Clams and oysters are molluscs with matching, two-part shells. Snails have a single shell.

A purple ring top snail creeps through orange cup corals in the northern Pacific Ocean.

Snails and Slugs

The great majority of molluscs are snails and slugs. Slugs are basically snails that have small, hidden shells or no shell at all.

Some kinds of sea slugs have bright, beautiful colors and forms. A snail without its shell looks very much like a slug. Many slugs and snails have two stalk-like **tentacles** on their heads. The tentacles help them sense movements and smells.

A Spanish shawl, a sea slug, is one of the brightest creatures in the sea.

Many Sizes

About half the 90,000 kinds of snails and slugs live in all the world's oceans, from the Arctic to the Antarctic.

The smallest sea snails are like grains of sand. The largest sea snails are the Australian baler and the Florida horse conch. The horse conch may be 2 feet (.61 meters) long! The horse conch has been Florida's state snail since 1969.

Florida's state snail, the horse conch, grows to be one of world's largest snails.

Getting Around

Whatever snails do, they do it slowly. This includes climbing, crawling, swimming, or burrowing.

Snails are built to last. Their kind has been with us for millions of years. But they're not built to be fast. They don't have wings or legs. Most of them do have a "foot."

Seen from below, an abalone shows off its muscular foot.

Washed ashore, this junonia is a prize for Florida shell hunters.

Too much collecting has made the beautiful queen conch scarce.

Snail Foot

A snail foot isn't the usual foot with toes. Instead, it's a fleshy muscle on the bottom side of the animal. It reaches from the shell to the surface beneath the snail.

The foot muscle makes wave-like motions. That allows the snail to move—slowly, of course.

A pair of olive snails use their feet to burrow into sand.

Predator and Prey

Some sea snails are **predators**. The tulip snail, fighting crown, and horse conch, for example, eat other molluscs. In some attacks, the snail's foot grasps the **prey**. Then the predator snail pokes its **proboscis** into the prey's flesh. The proboscis is like a small trunk with hard, sharp teeth at its tip.

The strong foot of a banded tulip snail is both a weapon and a means for crawling.

A cone snail uses **venom** from its proboscis to kill prey. Cone shell venom can even kill humans.

Some sea snails use their proboscis and its toothy edges to feed on plants.

Snails themselves are sometimes prey. Various seabirds, fish, sea turtles, and other molluscs eat snails.

This cone snail has a beautiful shell, but a deadly nature.

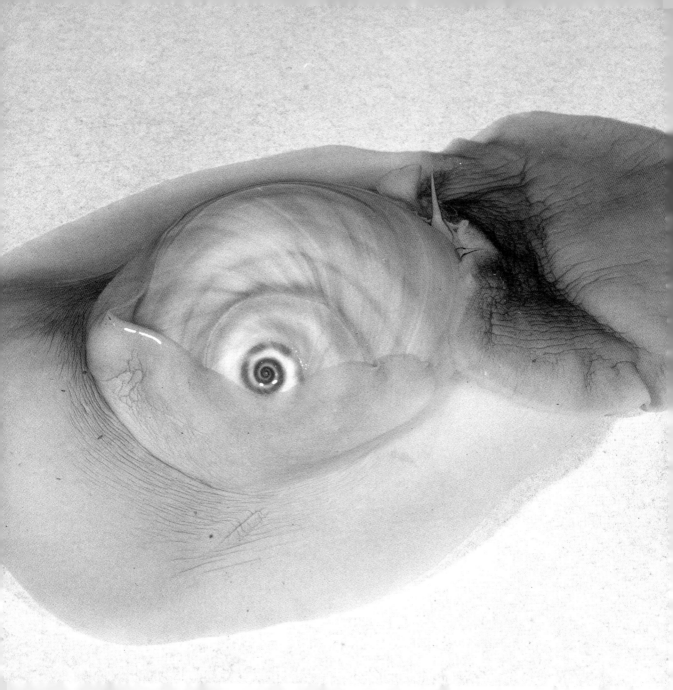

Snail Shells

Each snail has a thin layer of skin-like tissue called a **mantle**. The mantle releases liquid material that hardens into the snail's limestone shell. The shell grows as the snail grows. The large majority of snails have coiled shells that end in a sharp tip.

A moon snail spreads its slippery mantle.

Shells on the Shore

When a snail dies, its body **decays**, but its shell remains. There are snail shells along almost every seashore. Rare, beautiful shells, like junonias, are loved by collectors.

Empty snail shells are wonderful prizes. The collection of living sea snails, however, has made several kinds scarce.

Glossary

decays (dee KAYZ) — rots away

mantle (MAN tul) — a thin layer of skin-like flesh from which a snail produces its shell

molluscs (MAHL usks) — one group of related boneless animals, including many with shells, such as oysters, clams, and snails

predators (PRED eh torz) — animals that hunt other animals for food

prey (PRAY) — an animal hunted by other animals

proboscis (pro BOS ess) — a long, flexible snout, often used to suck, bite, or drill into

tentacles (TEN te kelz) — stalk-like structures on the heads of many snails and slugs; they are used to sense movement and smell

venom (VEN em) — animal poison usually used for both hunting and defense

Index

Further Reading

Holmes, Kevin J. *Snails*. Capstone, 1998
Pascoe, Elaine. *Snails and Slugs*. Gale Group, 1998
Wilkes, Angela. *Explore and Discover: Seashore*. Kingfisher, 2001

Websites To Visit

Queen Conch: http://www.enchantedlearning.com/subjects/inv
Shells and Conchology: http://www.seasky.org/links/sealink05.html/

About The Author

Lynn Stone is the author of more than 400 children's nonfiction books. He is a talented natural history photographer as well. Lynn, a former teacher, travels worldwide to photograph wildlife in its natural habitat.